The Astral Centers Or Chakras

Rudolf Steiner

Kessinger Publishing's Rare Reprints

Thousands of Scarce and Hard-to-Find Books on These and other Subjects!

- Americana
- Ancient Mysteries
- Animals
- Anthropology
- Architecture
- Arts
- Astrology
- Bibliographies
- Biographies & Memoirs
- Body, Mind & Spirit
- Business & Investing
- Children & Young Adult
- Collectibles
- Comparative Religions
- Crafts & Hobbies
- Earth Sciences
- Education
- Ephemera
- Fiction
- Folklore
- Geography
- Health & Diet
- History
- Hobbies & Leisure
- Humor
- Illustrated Books
- Language & Culture
- Law
- Life Sciences
- Literature
- Medicine & Pharmacy
- Metaphysical
- Music
- Mystery & Crime
- Mythology
- Natural History
- Outdoor & Nature
- Philosophy
- Poetry
- Political Science
- Science
- Psychiatry & Psychology
- Reference
- Religion & Spiritualism
- Rhetoric
- Sacred Books
- Science Fiction
- Science & Technology
- Self-Help
- Social Sciences
- Symbolism
- Theatre & Drama
- Theology
- Travel & Explorations
- War & Military
- Women
- Yoga
- *Plus Much More!*

We kindly invite you to view our catalog list at:
http://www.kessinger.net

I

THE ASTRAL CENTRES
(CHAKRAS)

IT is one of the essential principles of genuine occultism that he who devotes himself to a study of it should only do so with a complete understanding ; should neither undertake nor practise anything of which he does not realise the results. An occult teacher giving a person either instruction or counsel will invariably begin with an explanation of those changes in body, in soul, and in spirit, which will occur to him who seeks for the higher knowledge.

We shall consider here some of these

effects upon the soul of the occult student, for only he who is cognisant of what is now to be said can undertake with a full understanding the practices which will lead to a knowledge of the superphysical worlds. Indeed, one may say that it is only such who are genuine occult students. By true occultism all experimenting in the dark is very strongly discouraged. He who will not undergo with open eyes the period of schooling, may become a medium, but all such efforts cannot bring him to clairvoyance as it is understood by the occultist.

To those who, in the right way, have practised the methods (concerning the acquisition of superphysical knowledge) which were indicated in my book, entitled *The Way of Initiation*,[1] certain changes

---

[1] *The Way of Initiation, or How to Attain Knowledge of the Higher Worlds.* By Rudolf Steiner, Ph.D. With a foreword by Annie Besant, and some Biographical

occur in what is called "the astral body" (the organism of the soul). This organism is only perceptible to the clairvoyant. One may compare it to a more or less luminous cloud which is discerned in the midst of the physical body, and in this astral body the impulses, desires, passions, and ideas become visible. Sensual appetites, for example, are manifested as dark-red outpourings of a particular shape; a pure and noble thought is expressed in an outpouring of reddish-violet colour; the clear-cut conception of a logical thinker will appear as a yellow figure with quite sharp outlines; while the confused thought of a cloudy brain is manifested as a figure with vague out-lines. The thoughts of people with views that are one-sided and firmly fixed will

Notes of the Author by Edouard Schuré. Second impression. 237 pp. Cloth. Crown 8vo. 3s. 6d. net. Postage 4d. extra.

appear sharp in their outlines, but immobile; while those of people who remain accessible to other points of view are seen to be in motion, with varying outlines.

The further the student now advances in his psychic development, the more will his astral body become regularly organised; in the case of a person whose psychic life is undeveloped, it remains ill-organised and confused. Yet in such an unorganised astral body the clairvoyant can perceive a form which stands out clearly from its environment. It extends from the interior of the head to the middle of the physical body. It appears as, in a certain sense, an independent body possessed of special organs. These organs, which are now to be considered, are seen to exist in the following parts of the physical body: the first between the eyes; the second at the larynx; the third in the region of the heart; the fourth in what is called the pit of the stomach ; while the fifth and sixth are situated in the abdomen. Such forms are technically known as "wheels" (chakras) or "lotus-flowers." They are so called on account of their likeness to wheels or flowers, but of course it should be clearly understood that such an expression is not to be applied more literally than when one calls the lobes of the lungs the "wings." Just as everybody knows that here one is not really dealing with "wings," so must it be remembered that in respect of the "wheels" one is merely speaking figuratively. These "lotus-flowers" are at present, in the undeveloped person, of dark colours and without movement—inert. In the clairvoyant, however, they are seen to be in motion and of luminous colour. In the medium something similar happens, albeit in a different way ; but that part of the subject cannot now be pursued any further. As soon as the occult student begins his practices, the lotus-flowers first become lucent; later on they begin to revolve. It is when this occurs that the faculty of clairvoyance begins. For these "flowers" are the sense-organs of the soul, and their revolutions make manifest the fact that one is able to perceive in the superphysical world. No one can behold any superphysical thing until he has in this way developed his astral senses.

The sense-organ, which is situated in the vicinity of the larynx, allows one to perceive clairvoyantly the thoughts of another person, and also brings a deeper insight into the true laws of natural phenomena. The organ situated near the heart permits of a clairvoyant knowledge concerning the sentiments of another person. He who has developed it can also observe certain of the deeper powers in animals and plants. By means of the organ that lies in the pit of the stomach one acquires knowledge of the capacities and talents of a person : by this, too, one is enabled to see what parts in the household of nature are played by animals, plants, stones, metals, atmospheric phenomena, and so on.

The organ situated at the larynx has sixteen "petals" or "spokes"; that which is in the region of the heart has twelve; that which is in the pit of the stomach has ten. Now certain activities of the soul are connected with the development of these sense-organs, and he who practises them in a particular way contributes something to the development of the astral organs concerned. Eight of the sixteen petals of the "lotus" have been developed already during an earlier stage of human evolution, in a remote past. To this development the human being contributed nothing. He held them as a gift of Nature, when he was yet in a dreamy, dull state of consciousness. At that stage of human evolution they were already active. The manner of their activity, however, was only compatible with the dull state of consciousness already mentioned. As consciousness then grew brighter, the petals became obscure and withdrew their activity. The other eight can be developed by a person's conscious practice, and after that the entire lotus becomes both brilliant and active. The acquisition of certain capacities depends upon the development of everyone of these petals. Yet, as already shown, one can only consciously develop eight of them; the other eight reappear spontaneously.

Their development is consummated in the following manner. One must apply oneself with care and attention to certain functions of the soul which one usually

xercises in a careless manner and without
ttention.   There are eight such functions.
The first depends on the manner in which
ne receives ideas.   People usually allow
hemselves to be led in this respect by
hance alone.   They hear this and that,
hey see one thing and another, upon
which they base their ideas.   While this
s the case the sixteen petals of the lotus
emain quite torpid.   Only when one
egins in this matter to take one's educa-
ion into one's own hands do they really
egin to be effective.   All conceptions
must be guarded with this end in view.
Every idea should have some significance.
One ought to see in it a certain message,
 fragment of knowledge concerning the
hings of the outer world, and one must
ot be satisfied with conceptions that have
o such significance.   One should so
overn one's mental life that it becomes a
mirror of the outer world, and should

direct one's energies to the expulsion of incorrect ideas.

The second of these functions is concerned, in a similar way, with the control of the resolutions. One should only make resolutions after a well-founded, full consideration of even the most insignificant points. All thoughtless deeds, all meaningless actions, should be put far away from the soul. For everything one must have well-considered grounds, and one ought never to do a thing for which there is no real need.

The third function relates to speech. The occult student should only utter what is sensible and purposeful. All talking for the sake of talking draws him away from his path. He must avoid the usual method of conversation, in which all manner of things, unselected and heterogeneous, are spoken of together. In accomplishing this, however, he must not preclude himself from intercourse with his fellows. Precisely in such intercourse ought his conversation to grow in significance. He answers everybody, but he does so thoughtfully and after careful consideration of the question. He never speaks without grounds for what he says. He seeks to use neither too many nor too few words.

The fourth function is the regulation of outward action. The student seeks to direct his actions in such a way that it fits in with the actions of his fellow-men and with the peculiarities of his environment. He rejects all actions that are disturbing to others or that are antagonistic to those which are customary around him. He tries so to act that his deeds may combine harmoniously with his environment, with his position in life, and so forth. Where he is caused to act by some external suggestion he considers carefully how he can best respond. Where he is his own master, he considers the effects of his methods of action with the utmost care.

The fifth activity here to be noticed lies in the management of the entire life. The occult student endeavours to live in conformity with both Nature and Spirit. Never over-hasty, he is also never idle. Indolence and superfluous activity lie equally far away from him. He looks upon life as a means for work and he lives accordingly. He arranges habits, and fosters health so that a harmonious life is the outcome.

The sixth is concerned with human endeavour. The student tests his capacities and his knowledge and conducts himself in the light of such self-knowledge. He tries to perform nothing that is beyond his powers; but also to omit nothing for which they inwardly seem adequate. On the other hand, he sets before himself aims that coincide with the ideal, with the high duty of a human being. He does not merely regard himself half thoughtlessly as a wheel in the vast machinery of mankind, but endeavours to comprehend its problems, to look out beyond the trivial and the daily. He thus endeavours to fulfil his obligations ever better and more perfectly.

The seventh change in the life of his soul deals with the effort to learn as much from life as possible. Nothing passes before the student without giving him occasion to accumulate experience which is of value to him for life. If he has done anything wrongly or imperfectly, it offers an opportunity later on to make it correspondingly either right or perfect. If he sees others act, he watches them with a similar intent. He tries to collect from experience a rich treasure, and ever to consult it attentively; nor, indeed, will he do anything without having looked back over experiences that can give him help in his decisions and actions.

Finally, the eighth is this : the student must from time to time look inward, sink back into himself, take careful counsel with himself, build up and test the foundations of his life, run over his store of knowledge, ponder upon his duties, consider the contents and aim of life, and so forth. All these matters have already been mentioned in *The Way of Initiation* (see page 2); here they are merely recapitulated in connection with the development of the sixteen-petalled lotus. By means of these exercises it will become ever more and more perfect, for upon such practices depends the development of clairvoyance. For instance, the more what a person thinks and utters harmonises with the actual occurrences of the outer world, the more quickly will he develop this faculty. He who thinks or speaks

anything that is untrue kills something
in the bud of the sixteen-petalled lotus.
Truthfulness, Uprightness, and Honesty are
in this connection formative, but Falsehood,
Simulation, and Dishonesty are destructive
forces. The student must recognise that
not merely "good intentions" are needed,
but also actual deeds. If I think or say
anything which does not harmonise with
the truth, I kill something in my astral
organs, even although I believed myself
to speak or think from intentions ever so
good. It is here as with the child who
needs must burn itself if it falls into the
fire, even although this may have occurred
from ignorance. The regulation of the
above-mentioned activities of the soul in
the manner described, allows the sixteen-
petalled lotus to ray forth in splendid hues
and imparts to it a definite movement.
Yet it must be remarked that the signs of
clairvoyant faculty cannot appear before

a certain stage of this development is reached. So long as it is a trouble to lead this kind of life the faculty remains unmanifested. So long as one has to give special thought to the matters already described, one is yet unripe. Only when one has carried them so far that one lives quite habitually in the specified manner can the preliminary traces of clairvoyance appear. These matters must therefore no longer seem troublesome, but must become the habitual way of life. There is no need to watch oneself continually, nor to force oneself on to such a life. Everything must become habitual. There are certain instructions by the fulfilment of which the lotus may be brought to blossom in another way. But such methods are rejected by true occultism, for they lead to the destruction of physical health and to the ruin of morality. They are easier to accomplish than those described, which re protracted and troublesome, but the latter lead to the true goal and cannot but strengthen morality. (The student will notice that the spiritual practices described above correspond to what is called in Buddhism " the eightfold path." Here the connection between that path and the upbuilding of the astral organs must be explained.)

If to all that has been said there is added the observance of certain orders which the student may only receive orally from the teacher, there results an acceleration in the development of the sixteen-petalled lotus. But such instructions cannot be given outside the precincts of an occult school. Yet the regulation of life in the way described is also useful for those who will not, or cannot, attach themselves to a school. For the effect upon the astral body occurs in every case, even if it be but slowly. To the occult pupil

2

the observance of these principles is indispensable. If he should try to train himself in occultism without observing them, he could only enter the higher world with defective mental eyes; and in place of knowing the truth he would then be merely subject to deception and illusion. In a certain direction he might become clairvoyant; but fundamentally nothing but a blindness completer than of old would beset him. For hitherto he stood at least firmly in the midst of the sense-world and had in it a certain support; but now he sees beyond that world and will fall into error concerning it before he is able to stand securely in a higher sphere. As a rule, indeed, he cannot distinguish error from truth, and he loses all direction in life. For this very reason is patience in such matters essential. It must always be remembered that the occult teacher may not proceed very far with his instructions unless an earnest desire for a regulated development of the lotus - flowers is already present. Only mere caricatures of these flowers could be evolved if they were brought to blossom before they had acquired, in a steady manner, their appropriate form. For the special instructions of the teacher bring about the blossoming of the lotuses, but form is imparted to them by the manner of life already outlined. The irregular development of a lotus-flower has, for its result, not only illusion and fantastic conceptions where a certain kind of clairvoyance has occurred, but also errors and lack of balance in life itself. Through such development one may well become timid, envious, conceited, self-willed, stiff-necked, and so on, while hitherto one may have possessed none of these characteristics. It has already been said that eight petals of the lotus were developed long ago, in a very remote past, and that these in the course of occult education unfold again of themselves. In the instruction of the student, all care must now be given to the other eight. By erroneous teaching the former may easily appear alone, and the latter remain untended and inert. This would be the case particularly when too little logical, reasonable thinking is introduced into the instruction. It is of supreme importance that the student should be a sensible and clear-thinking person, and of equal importance that he should practise the greatest clarity of speech. People who begin to have some presentiment of superphysical things are apt to become talkative about such things. In that way they retard their development. The less one talks about these matters the better. Only he who has come to a certain stage of clearness ought to speak of them.

At the commencement of the instructions occult students are astonished, as a rule, to find how little curiosity the teacher exhibits concerning their experiences. It were best of all for them if they were to remain entirely uncommunicative about these experiences, and should say nothing further than how successful or how unsuccessful they had been in the performance of their exercises or in the observance of their instructions. The occult teacher has quite other means of estimating their progress than their own communications. The eight petals now under consideration always become a little hardened through such communication where they ought really to grow soft and supple. An illustration shall be given to explain this, not taken from the superphysical world, but, for the sake of clearness, from ordinary life. Suppose that I hear a piece of news and thereupon form at once an opinion. In a little while I receive

some further news which does not harmonise with the previous information. I
am constrained thereby to reverse my
original judgment. The result of this is an
unfavourable influence upon my sixteen-
petalled lotus. It would have been quite
otherwise if, in the first place, I had sus-
pended my judgment; if concerning the
whole affair I had remained, inwardly in
thought and outwardly in words, entirely
silent until I had acquired quite reliable
grounds for the formation of my judgment.
Caution in the formation and the pro-
nouncement of opinions becomes, by
degrees, the special characteristic of the
occult student. Thereby he increases
his sensibility to impressions and experiences, which he allows to pass over him
silently in order to collect the largest possible number of facts from which to form
his opinions. There exist in the lotus-
flower bluish-red and rose-red shades of

colour which manifest themselves under the influence of such circumspection, while in the opposite case orange and dark red shades would appear.

The twelve-petalled lotus which lies in the region of the heart is formed in a similar way. Half its petals, likewise, were already existent and active in a remote stage of human evolution. These six petals do not require to be especially evolved in the occult school: they appear spontaneously and begin to revolve when we set to work on the other six. In the cultivation of these, as in the previous case, one has to control and direct certain activities of the mind in a special way.

It must be clearly understood that the perceptions of each astral or soul-organ bear a peculiar character. The twelve-petalled lotus possesses perception of quite a different kind from that of the sixteen petals. The latter perceives forms. The

thoughts of a person and the laws under
which a natural phenomenon takes place
appear to the sixteen-petalled lotus as
forms—not, however, rigid, motionless
forms, but active and filled with life. The
clairvoyant, in whom this sense is well
evolved, can discern a form wherewith
every thought, every natural law, finds
expression. A thought of vengeance, for
example, manifests as an arrowlike, pronged
form, while a thought of goodwill fre-
quently takes the shape of an opening
flower. Clear-cut, meaningful thoughts
are formed regularly and symmetrically,
while hazy conceptions take on hazy outlines. By means of the twelve-petalled
flower quite different perceptions are
acquired. Approximately one can indi-
cate the nature of these perceptions by
likening them to the sense of cold and
heat. A clairvoyant equipped with this
faculty feels a mental warmth or chilliness

raying out from the forms discerned by
means of the sixteen-petalled flower. If a
clairvoyant had evolved the sixteen-petalled
lotus, but not the lotus of twelve petals, he
would only observe a thought of goodwill
as the shape already described, while another in whom both senses were developed
would also discern that outraying of the
thought which one can only call a mental
warmth.   It may be remarked in passing
that in the occult school one sense is never
evolved without the other, so that what has
just been said should only be regarded as
having been stated for the sake of clarity.
By the cultivation of the twelve-petalled
lotus the clairvoyant discovers in himself a
deep comprehension of natural processes.
Everything that is growing or evolving
rays out warmth ; everything that is decay-
ng, perishing, or in ruins, will seem cold.

The development of this sense may be
accelerated in the following manner. The

first requirement is that the student should
apply himself to the regulation of his
thoughts. Just as the sixteen-petalled lotus
achieves its evolution by means of earnest
and significant thinking, so is the twelve-
petalled flower cultivated by means of an
inward control over the currents of thought.
Errant thoughts which follow each other
in no logical or reasonable sequence, but
merely by pure chance, destroy the form
of the lotus in question. The more one
thought follows another, the more all dis-
connected thought is thrown aside, the
more does this astral organ assume its
appropriate form. If the student hears
illogical thought expressed, he should
silently set it straight within his own
mind. He ought not, for the purpose of
perfecting his own development, to with-
draw himself uncharitably from what is
perhaps an illogical mental environment.
Neither should he allow himself to feel

impelled to correct the illogical thinking around him.   Rather should he quietly, in his own inner self, constrain this whirl-pool of thoughts to a logical and reasonable course.   And above all things ought he to strive after this regulation in the region of his own thoughts.

A second requirement is that he should control his actions in a similar way.   All instability or disharmony of action produces a withering effect upon the lotus- · flower which is here in consideration.   If the student has done anything he should manage the succeeding act so that it forms a logical sequence to the first, for he who acts differently from day to day will never evolve this faculty or sense.

· The third requirement is the cultivation ⸳ of perseverance.   The occult student never allows himself to be drawn by this or that influence aside from his goal so long as he continues to believe that it is the right one.

Obstacles are for him like challenges to overcome them and never afford reasons for loitering on the way.

The fourth requirement is tolerance as regards all persons and circumstances. The student should seek to avoid all superfluous criticism of imperfections and vices, and should rather endeavour to comprehend everything that comes under his notice.   Even as the sun does not refuse its light to the evil and the vicious, so he, too, should not refuse them an intelligent sympathy.   If the student meets with some trouble, he should not waste his force in criticism, but bow to necessity and seek how he may try to transmute the misfortune into good.   He does not look at another's opinions from his own standpoint alone, but seeks to put himself into his companion's position.

The fifth requirement is impartiality in one's relation to the affairs of life.   In this

connection we speak of "trust" and "faith."
The occult student goes out to every person and every creature with this faith, and
through it he acts. He never says to himself, when anything is told to him, " I do
not believe that, since it is opposed to
my present opinions." Far rather is
he ready at any moment to test and
rearrange his opinions and ideas. He
always remains impressionable to everything that confronts him. Likewise does
he trust in the efficiency of what he
undertakes. Timidity and scepticism are
banished from his being. If he has any
purpose in view, he has also faith in its
power. A hundred failures cannot rob
him of this confidence. It is indeed that
" faith which can move mountains."

The sixth requirement is the cultivation
of a certain equanimity. The student
strives to temper his moods, whether they
come laden with sorrow or with joy. He

must avoid the extremes of rising up to
the sky in rapture or sinking down to the
earth in despair, but should constantly
control his mind and keep it evenly
balanced. Sorrow and peril, joy and
prosperity alike find him ready armed.

The reader of theosophical literature
will find the qualities here described,
under the name of the "six attributes"
which must be striven after by him who
would attain to initiation. Here their
connection with the astral sense, which
is called the twelve-petalled lotus, is to
be explained. The teacher can impart
specific instructions which cause the
lotus to blossom; but here, as before, the
development of its symmetrical form
depends upon the attributes already mentioned. He who gives little or no heed
to that development will only form this
organ into a caricature of its proper shape.
It is possible to cultivate a certain clair-

voyance of this nature by directing these attributes to their evil side instead of to the good. A person may be intolerant, faint-hearted, and contentious toward his environment; may, for instance, perceive the sentiments of other people and either run away from them or hate them. This can be so accentuated that on account of the mental coldness which rays out to him from opinions which are contrary to his own, he cannot bear to listen to them, or else behaves in an objectionable manner.

The mental culture which is important for the development of the ten-petalled lotus is of a peculiarly delicate kind, for here it is a question of learning to dominate, in a particular manner, the very sense-impressions themselves. It is of especial importance to the clairvoyant at the outset, for only by this faculty can he avoid a source of countless illusions and mental mirages. Usually, a person is not at all

clear as to what things have dominion
over his memories and fancies. Let us
take the following case. Someone travels
on the railway, and busies himself with
a thought. Suddenly his thoughts take
quite another direction. He then recol-
lects an experience which he had some
years ago, and interweaves it with his
immediate thought. But he did not notice
that his eyes have been turned toward the
window, and were caught by the glance
of a person who bears a likeness to someone else who was intimately concerned
with the recollected experience. He
remains unconscious of what he has seen
and is only conscious of the results, and
he therefore believes that the whole affair
arose spontaneously. How much in life
occurs in such a way! We play over
things in our lives which we have read or
experienced without bringing the connection into our consciousness. Some one,

for instance, cannot bear a particular colour, but he does not realise that this is due to the fact that the school-teacher of whom he was afraid, many years ago, used to wear a coat of that colour. Innumerable illusions are based upon such associations. Many things penetrate to the soul without becoming embodied in the consciousness. The following case is a possible example. Some one reads in the paper about the death of a well-known person, and straightway is convinced that yesterday he had a presentiment about it, although he neither saw nor heard of anything that could have given rise to such a thought. It is quite true, the thought that this particular person would die, emerged yesterday "by itself," only he has failed to notice one thing. Two or three hours before this thought occurred to him yesterday he went to visit an acquaintance. A newspaper lay on the

table, but he did not read it. Yet unconsciously his eyes fell upon an account of
the dangerous illness in which the person
concerned was lying. He was not conscious of the impression, but the effects of
it were, in reality, the whole substance of
the " presentiment."

If one reflects upon such matters, one
can measure how deep a source of illusion
and fantasy they supply. It is this that
he who desires to foster the ten-petalled
lotus must dam up, for by means of the
latter one can perceive characteristics
deeply embedded in human and other
beings. But the truth can only be
extracted from these perceptions if one
has entirely freed oneself from the delu-
sions here described. For this purpose
it is necessary that one should become
master of that which is carried in to
one from the external world. One must
extend this mastery so far that veritably

one does not receive those influences which one does not desire to receive, and this can only be achieved gradually by living a very powerful inward life. This must be so thoroughly done that one only allows those things to impress one on which one voluntarily directs the attention, and that one really prevents those impressions which might otherwise be unconsciously registered. What is seen must be voluntarily seen, and that to which no attention is given must actually no longer exist for oneself. The more vitally and energetically the soul does its inward work, the more will it acquire this power. The occult student must avoid all vague wanderings of sight or hearing. For him only those things to which he turns his eye or his ear must exist. He must practise the power of hearing nothing even in the loudest disturbance when he wishes to hear nothing : he must render his eyes unimpressionable to things which he does not especially desire to notice. He must be shielded as by a mental armour from all unconscious impressions. But in the region of his thoughts particularly must he apply himself in this respect. He puts a thought before him and only seeks to think such thoughts as, in full consciousness and freedom, he can relate to it. Fancy he rejects. If he finds himself anxious to connect one thought with another, he feels round carefully to discover how this latter thought occurred to him. He goes yet further. If, for instance, he has a particular antipathy for anything, he will wrestle with it and endeavour to find out some conscious connection between the antipathy and its object. In this way the unconscious elements in his soul become ever fewer and fewer. Only by such severe self-searching can the ten-petalled lotus attain

he form which it ought to possess. The
mental life of the occult student must be
an attentive life, and he must know how
to ignore completely everything which he
does not wish, or ought not, to observe.

If such introspection is followed by a
meditation, which is prescribed by the
instructions of the teacher, the lotus-
flower in the region of the pit of the
stomach blossoms in the correct way, and
that which had appeared (to the astral
senses already described) as form and heat
acquires also the characteristics of light
and colour. Through this are revealed,
for instance, the talents and capacities of
people, the powers and the hidden attributes of Nature. The coloured aura of
the living creature then becomes visible;
all that is around us then manifests its
spiritual attributes. It will be obvious
that the very greatest care is necessary
in the development of this province, for

the play of unconscious memories is here exceedingly active. If this were not the case, many people would possess the sense now under consideration, for it appears almost immediately if a person has really got the impressions of his senses so completely under his power that they depend on nothing but his attention or inattention. Only so long as the dominion of the senses holds the soul in subjection and dullness, does it remain inactive.

Of greater difficulty than the development of this lotus is that of the six-petalled flower which is situated in the centre of the body. For to cultivate this it is necessary to strive after a complete mastery of the whole personality by means of self-consciousness, so that body, soul, and spirit make but one harmony. The functions of the body, the inclinations and passions of the soul, the thoughts and ideas of the spirit must be brought into com-

lete union with each other. The body
must be so refined and purified that its
organs assimilate nothing which may not
be of service to the soul and spirit. The
soul must assimilate nothing through the
body, whether of passion or desire, which
is antagonistic to pure and noble thoughts.
The spirit must not dominate the soul
with laws and obligations like a slave-
owner, but rather must the soul learn to
follow by inclination and free choice these
laws and duties. The duties of an occult
student must not rule him as by a power
to which he unwillingly submits, but rather
as by something which he fulfils because
he likes it. He must evolve a free soul
which has attained an equilibrium between
sense and spirit. He must carry this so
far that he can abandon himself to the
sense because it has been so ennobled that
it has lost the power to drag him down.
He must no longer require to curb his

passions, inasmuch as they follow the good by themselves. As long as a person has to chastise himself he cannot arrive at a certain stage of occult education, for a virtue to which one has to constrain oneself is then valueless. As long as one retains a desire, even although one struggles not to comply therewith, it upsets one's development, nor does it matter whether this appetite be of the soul or of the body. For example, if some one avoids a particular stimulant for the purpose of purifying himself by refining his pleasures, it can only benefit him if his body suffers nothing by this deprivation. If this be not the case it is an indication that the body requires the stimulant, and the renunciation is then worthless. In this case it may even be true that the person in question must first of all forego the desirable goal and wait until favourable conditions—perhaps only in another life—

shall surround him.   A tempered renunciation is, under certain circumstances, a
much greater acquisition than the struggle
for something which in given conditions
remains unattainable.   Indeed, such a
tempered renunciation contributes more
than such struggle to one's development.

He who has evolved the six-petalled
lotus can communicate with beings who
are native to the higher worlds, though
even then only if their presence is manifested in the astral or soul-world.   In an
occult school, however, no instructions
concerning the development of this lotus-
flower would be imparted before the
student had trodden far enough on the
upward path to permit of his spirit
mounting into a yet higher world.   The
formation of these lotus-flowers must
always be accompanied by entrance into
this really spiritual sphere.   Otherwise
the student would fall into error and

uncertainty. He would undoubtedly be able to see, but he would remain incapable of estimating rightly the phenomena there seen. Now there already exists in him who has learned to evolve the six-petalled lotus, a security from error and giddiness, for no one who has acquired complete equilibrium of sense (or body), passion (or soul), and thought (or spirit) will be easily led into mistakes. Nothing is more essential than this security when, by the development of the six-petalled lotus, beings possessed of life and independence, and belonging to a world so completely hidden from his physical senses, are revealed before the spirit of the student. In order to ensure the necessary safety in this world, it is not enough to have cultivated the lotus-flowers, since he must have yet higher organs at his disposal.

CPSIA information can be obtained
at www.ICGtesting.com
Printed in the USA
BVHW042020180621
609918BV00014B/481